Sonofabitch Poems

Poems by R L Raymond

Sonofabitch Poems

First Edition

Printed in Canada

PigeonBike Press

ISBN - 978-0-9869509-0-2

PigeonBike Press – Canada – 2011
www.PigeonBike.com
PigeonBike@bell.net

Acknowledgments

A special tip o' the hat to John Yamrus who has read, helped and motivated me to put this little book together.

Thanks also to Lavonne Westbrooks for her careful and invaluable proofreading and suggestions.

RLR

Dedicated to all the non-poets

Contents

A human whelping box

she was almost asleep
in the king-size bed
breathing slowly
nuzzling their daughter close
desperate to name the scent floating from her fontanel

the argument replayed in her mind:
she said it would keep their little one from crying –
warm contact and the rhythm of her heartbeat –
just like she learned in childcare books and on afternoon TV

he totally disagreed
and she cursed him…
disgusted by his smug comment about the Spartans
that she wasn't a damn puppy
absolutely horrified that he had said she would smother her

he slept alone
in the guest bedroom
dreaming about his baby girl that smelled of cinnamon

A dirty bowl

the dry well echoes
hollow
every sunday afternoon
with a coin secretly
palmed from the
collection plate
the tinny reverb plinked
stone-bounced
all the way down
to the dirt
in the empty bucket
inside

eyes closed
the child mutters
amid cicada shells
twice-dead and desiccated
picked from nearby trees
spiraling castanet
on the backs of
dust witches
dancing at his feet

the old man
startles him
fingering ash
from the bowl of his pipe
looking at his boots
speckled whitish-grey –

kid they all look for water
before they die
you're just wasting
your time
          and that money
wishing her back
she won't come –
you may as well've been
praying for rain

La chasse-galerie

sac-à-tabi
sac-à-tabac
she'd sent him out
for smokes

the *dépanneur*
was next
to the catholic
church

she'd told him
clear as day
no chats with
the *prêtre*

the sun setting
she fretted
not with worry
but anger

he'd borrowed
her car that little bastard
promised the
left over change

if he'd stopped
at *l'église*
he'd come home
to the real devil

Exhaust on the wildflowers

he races through
the swarm of night flies
parting the lucky ones
to the side
the others
streak-clicking
against the glass
wiper smeared
the emptied husks
twirling behind
in a vortex
of burnt diesel
and dust

a bottle tossed
from the window
whistles over
the redline whine
then shatters
amid the cattails

sure he had
forgotten

and she had not

but would she
when the bouquets
limped

when the fiddleheads
straightened then
shook away
the filth
of beetles and
broken glass

On the road...

a traveller
rudely awakened by the sun's right hook
sickened by the virulence of his breath
prisoner in over-starched white bedding
spits out the first word that comes to his mind
"Clusterfuck" through pursed lips and hairy teeth
wondering aloud just for a second
if the meaning carries the same weight as
it did at home

A little yellow room

maybe he hadn't heard her scream 'no!'
because her voice was young
and again
maybe he hadn't heard her scream 'I'm bleeding!'
because the phone lines were scratchy

she hailed the cab alone
so mom wouldn't find out

saint christopher looked at her from the dash
hopefully he'd help the driver get her to the ER

the back seat stank of businessmen
and drunks and stupid tourists

she closed her eyes to block it out
imagining a little yellow room
from a hallmark special around christmas time
where girls in pigtails and boys with perfectly parted hair
were polite and beautiful
singing songs about baby jesus

Officer & Gentleman

she wanted diamonds
warmed in polar bear fur
never tainted by blood

the hand-carved bit of ebony
bought from the street vendor
near the coffee shop where they first met

felt thin and insignificant
in his vest breast pocket
her wish negating its meaning

***

the pimp took the beating stoically
just like he expected from his girls
spitting a smiled insult through his grills

the heavy gold two-fingered ring
chosen for flash and damage quotient
bypassed the evidence bag into his vest pocket

hidden behind the bodega
the cop threw one last punch
straight into his face

wondering
who could reset
the stones into earrings

On the grate

She stared from her exhaust and spit streaked tarp
trapping the city's flatulent heat close
watching him stroll
backlit film-noir
to her corner

One thanksgiving so many years ago
everyone had made her blush with pride
when they toasted
her engagement
to the doctor

After it had all fallen asunder
through god's harsh will or her drinking binges
he pitched her out
a lapse in judgment
to be forgotten

But this night he finally came for her
approaching through the steam and rum rancor
of her breathing
for forgiveness…
and just walked on

Old Bellerophon

looking down through the kaleidoscope
he pretended that they were
rubies placed about her head
a tiara fit for Anteia

smoke roiled from the silver champagne bucket
the leather cover of the little book charred
burned paper carrying each name
to Hades on the wings of her lies

he flicked a sparkle of glass from his glove
dropped the zippo in his trenchcoat pocket
other hand around the pistol
still warm from the lead he'd put in her gut

he calmly left the room
feeling the curse of age gnaw at his bones

Lucky Luke

The bumper sticker reads
crucify a tailgater
and he chuckles at the irony
of the small font on the chrome

and just then his car fills with red
amplified by the thick mist
spraying off the pavement –
he doesn't even get to enjoy his well-timed "*christ...*"

a tap of the brake pedal
tosses him sideways
off the backs of the parallel
snakes he'd been riding

breath slow
hands grip
wheels slip
onto the wet shoulder then off

but he's surprised by the gentleness
of the ditch
caressing the car onto its side
then tipping it back onto all fours

maybe the damage is minimal
maybe he'll be lucky for once

red dilutes pink from backup lights
as the pickup creeps to the edge
light clouds in the drizzle
then off

thin and nimble
the silhouette sidesteps down the slope
and jogs to the window
tapping it with a heavy ring

he rolls it down
I think I'll be fine
getting drenched
squinting…

the fist
hard and fast
nails him square
in the jaw

my dad's in the truck, prick…
nothing more
he leaps up the slope
taillights flash and fade

he sits
  face bloody
    sirens blare
      in the distance

At the beheading of crossdressers

blood boiled down
from spearpoints
into frozen sand

the hard iced earth
boiled down blood
to its separate parts

one was life one was honour
another surely flammable
down blood boiled

his cloak glowed bright red
in the farmhouse cinders
under the pink wisps
of melted snow

ref. Njal's Saga

Skallagrim

he was bald and beardless
and so goddamn tough
tough as nails
axe-dulling tough

he stole my beer once
much to my protests
protests weren't his thing
he shoved them up my ass my protests

another time he eyed my woman
such a pure beauty
beauty he wanted
and like my beer he drank that beauty

I hated him
hated him to death
death I dreamt about
but thirsty and alone I wasn't in the mood to deal in death

Gambrinus

Perched on the barstool
on crossed feet to look taller
he downed another pint
smacked down the mug

When he wanted to
      if push came to shove
           if the shit hit the fan
he could really mix it up

A low centre of gravity
fists as fat as hams
and an acumen buoyed
on barley and hops

He'd left the crown
on the bookshelf...
tonight was about drinking
and whatever else came his way

Vitus – just Vitus – nothing more

Not many men danced anymore
especially not in this type of joint
where thugs would rather stare and spit
than ask your name and shake your hand

Red wine stained his satin cuffs
poet sleeves as they were apt to call them
but he was lost to the rhythm
and the women fawning about

Yet all the while he never took his eyes from the bar
where they sat
      eyeballing him
           and smirking
the little fat one with a nose like a pig
and the bald one with the arse-of-a-babe face

He'd learned long ago not to mess with this type
the tough guy *sonofabitches*
out for a buzz
      out for a broad
           out for some blood
the type that never danced – at least not in public

L'acadien perdu

born and raised
in the stink of cigarettes and fish guts
making his name fighting
english boys in school yards
and years later
à leur peter la gueule
in strip clubs and dive bars

half a pint from passing out
he'd belched that he'd bought a plane
a chuckle cost a bloody tooth
a rolled eye turned black

the pretty girl from a town away
kissed his crooked smile
as she always did
through the *alcool* sting
falling asleep spooned at his side
proud of her *pilote*

they joked he was so tough
he could land it
half pissed
on the back of a moose

she said to stay
and they could drink
and screw
and forget about the storm

it was the only brawl he'd ever lost
when dusk had curled its shady fingers into fists
and wind had snuck up from behind
a sucker punch knocking him down
into the trackless snow

in spring the meltwaters bore him back
his essence an oilslick
in the gutters
of schools and bars and wanting homes

I have no filters *(for John Yamrus)*

he spoke through cigar smoke
thick as tear gas

but then again
filters are for
women's cigarettes
and american coffee

he spewed another cloud

pass me the obits
I wanna see who
the lucky bastards were

Edgeless

thunder-heavy snow
hides every contrast
of the frozen yard
boxwoods flattened
the drive erased

the ice cube cleaves in his tumbler

his choleric snarl hangs
in the breath-mist
solid and stagnant
over the rim of his glass

he'll have to shovel again tomorrow

another slug
another curse
against the snow
against the ice
and just against

I hate the city

tossing
bundles of newspaper
& flyers for
random things
tied with twine
to the curb

soda cans flattened
bottles crushed
orange juice
     soup tins
         & saltines…

he mumbles
I'm sick of this garbage
the sorting
the hauling
the stacking
the stench…

a neighbor pops out
his earphones
looks up from sweeping
cigarette butts
& candybar wrappers
from the gutter

"What?"

I said I hate the city…

"Then move."

After the third beer and not much to eat

he knew he'd been dead wrong
forgetting his own rule:
don't ask the questions
if you don't want the answers

***

It was harder to concentrate
when I was a kid

he looked up
from his black-thumbed
copy of En Attendant Godot
over his glasses

The clock actually ticked
and the furnace
made one hell of a racket

***

orange juice lost its cool sting
quickly
eggs not perfectly timed
turned greenish-grey
where the white
and the yolk
touched

he took notes he'd never read
on bills he'd never pay
not because of money
but ignorance

***

solitaire

A

K   K   K
Q   Q   Q
  J   J
   10   10
   9

grew to be a state of mind
and the cards
wouldn't cooperate

***

Maybe it's that I miss
that tick tick tick…
Maybe it was comfort
more than distraction
something always there
in the background
reminding you

"hey I'm here"
even though you only looked
two or three times a day…

***

long fingernails hardened yellow
made easy work of cracking sunflower seeds

Hulls too tough for
the old brittle teeth
but oh that little chunk of meat…

***

What upset him most
some days
were the stupid little things
he forgot
like cutting a notch in the
bologna
before frying it
and using a pat of butter
not oil
chewing the stale bread
and over-black
out-of-shape slab
slathered in mustard to cover
the burnt taste
he'd let his mind wander
to her

to anything
but this poor excuse of a sandwich

***

I finished the book
he looked across the table
still littered with
peels
  and shells
    and crumbly bits of bread
and every time I finish it
I expect something different
something new

I'll probably need
a shower soon too

The young woman
placed a brown bag
grease-spotted at its base
next to a gallon-sized cup

"It's iced tea
not sweet tea"

And a hamburger
with fries?

The young woman
nodded and sat across
from him

hands folded
on her knees
rubbing her thumbs

"What did you ever say
to make her leave?"

I just asked her a question:
Why do you stay?
Then another:
What's keeping you here?

She answered the first with silence
and the second with a door slam.
You know damn well
what happened next.

***

The old man leaned back
in his lounger
in his stink
listening to the click
of the springs

I haven't read Krapp's Last Tape
in a while
and can you get me a beer?
twist it open for me –
the old hands aren't what
they used to be

28

Whorefare

ice crackles electric snaps
in hidden timbers
mimicking the bottle caps
he flicks against the wall

cold contractions
through window and door
bleed white
from the witch outside

her sharp fingers etching
       prying
              scraping
to join the bitch within

fire bellied
       asleep fetal
              deaf to him
and his flick-clicking

hands astench of brass
small bills and coins
he takes one pull on the bottle
middle finger raised in salute

the living room is coldest
the couch beer-damp

the witch howls
the bitch snores

maybe a nailpop will wake him
      and one of them
            holding a gun
will smile

Progression

the old dog
      snarls toothless
      at the flashing hand

barks feebly
      as cars splash
      too close

but scans
      all-the-while
      through cataracts

for intercession
      or guidance
      from the little white man

Early onset

loaded for bear
she'd say
when he paced
upstairs

and we'd wait
at the table
his dinner long cold
hoping

he'd never find the key
to the gunsafe
so well hidden
in the cookie jar

Phenoptosis

Cheap wine spilt
on a floral tablecloth
puddles burgundy
under blue strobes
red under red

The megaphone blares
promises and demands
from officers
      and family
           and professionals

There has only been one shot
from the old house
with the perfect lawn
looping on the local TV station

None of them realize
he's roared his answer
to everyone
skywards
on a belch of cordite

Untitled – for and from MBC

the archangel Michael
hoped no one would notice
that he'd dropped his sword
not once
  not twice
    but three times
but he knew damn well
that Gabriel
wouldn't pass up an opportunity
to trumpet it to everyone

Crusts

he wheezed
ribeye
through teeth too spaced
in gums too weak
accompanied by the devil's tattoo
tapped
on the tarnished tube-rail
of the bed

ribeye
he hadn't had for years
the clicking of his yellow nail
worse than the cheap
clock on the nightstand

holding their breath
they air kissed him
once on each cheek

repeating his wish
he watched them leave
dipping a spoon in tapioca

———

hers had been closed
    too hard to cover
    the shattered socket
    outened eye
    and shifted nose

———

they don't sew 'em anymore

glued and waxed
his still lips quiet
under powdered makeup

they air kissed him
once on each cheek
in the casket

———

beside a picture
of the both of them
    when they were young
    with good teeth
    and happy faces
there was a plate
of cucumber sandwiches
with the crusts
cut off

no one ate a thing

Gravedigger – a long poem

Rough wind, that moanest loud
Grief too sad for song;
Wild wind, when sullen cloud
Knells all the night long;
Sad storm, whose tears are vain,
Bare woods, whose branches strain,
Deep caves and dreary main, –
Wail, for the world's wrong!

"A Dirge", Percy Bysshe Shelley, 1822

***

the fence was old
well built
six by six posts
one inch pine boards
but like the twigs and
wrist-thick branches strewn
about the yard
it may as well have been
matchsticks
in face of the storm

two sections lay on the grass
splintered slats and braces
torn from the broken post
snapped at the dirt line
a stub poking
from the ground
like a yellow tooth
in a rotten gum

he'd slept through it
however fitfully
the wind infiltrating
board and baton
through any warp
       or wow
creaking his house to
the very foundation
moaning its promise
of breakage

now he crawled
along with morning
through heat
stagnant and tangible
       all traces
       of cool
       or comfort
       or breeze
dead from the gale
scraping sleep and sweat
from his eyes

he saw the broken fence
the hole grinning

he raked the inconsequential
damage into piles
the unbroken boards were
stacked
by the shed
to be reused
stripped of their bent nails

the minor tasks done
he traded rake
for shovel
begrudging the chore
of pulling the stump

***

dust rose
suspended
particulate in the viscous calm
sticking
with each strike
to his hands and face

he drove through the sand
the clay
the pea-gravel
hacking at the bigger stones
the fist-sized ones

punching rust from the spade
exposing old silver
rolling the edge he'd faithfully
kept sharp

it took nearly an hour
to expose two feet
of the six by six
to loosen the rough concrete
footing
with boot kicks and phlegm globs
a chain and the pickup
would finish the job

he leaned
chin on hands
atop the weatherworn handle
resting
gazing at the cattails
arrow-straight
across the way
suddenly spotting a glint
of colour
of movement
nearly imperceptible
through the haze-shimmer
in the burned out field
not the usual children scaring
crows or chasing grasshoppers
no life
in what he saw

he walked
focusing on details
revealing themselves
        checkered hunting jacket
        grey hair
        maybe a pack
he called out
approaching
a supplicant on bent knees
silent

he shouted again
        an old man
turned
        his worn face
for an instant
        before returning to prayer

it wasn't a pack

he heard the flies
from a dozen paces
droning at the carcass
before the old man

drawn by the gravity
he saw the tatters
flaps of fur of blood of dirt

and the flies

my dog
damn wind blew the gate open
she weren't no hunter
not a chance against them coyotes

he took in this death
throat ripped
      removed
rear legs at wrong angles
      flesh punctured
eyes filmed cataract-like
      but worse
muzzle snarled
      lips torn
the teeth revealed yellow and red and black

and the flies

blue eyes swell-rimmed
and leather skin tear-streaked
when she didn't show up last night
I knew it wasn't gonna end well

he held back the clichés
platitudes and lies
mouthing *I'm sorry*
ashamed of its insignificance

***

chuck

      chuck

         chuck

the pine boards
clacked together
in the truck bed
then the shovel
and a piece of tarp
cut to size with his Case knife

at first the old man
refused
then reconsidered
unable to leave her there
alone
unable to carry her
a few miles
through the lea
with his bad leg

they built the stretcher
in the field
used it to heave
the ungiving mass
into the pickup

they didn't speak
much
bouncing down the country road
a few cursory details

down the way
a widower
just a daughter long gone

and it ended
abruptly
signalling the trespass
into no-man's land

it was a quaint farmhouse
well maintained
deepset at the long drive's end
lined with cedar hedges
the parterre dotted
with rock gardens
weeded and tended
abloom with stock still lilies

they unloaded the corpse
pall-borne away from
the stones of the drive
onto the dry
yellowing grass

I'd offer you a drink
but you understand
it's somethin' a man's gotta do
on his own

***

he watched him in the rearview

the old man dragged his dog
a little ways
limping
before disappearing
into the house

gravel pinged the wheelwells

***

crows broke at the shot
flying from their shady haunts

***

skids across the lawn
sidestepping the carcass
he'd just left
but shouldn't have

inside
the farmhouse
was neat
a picture that should
have smelled of apple pie
not
an old man on the floor
of the kitchen
leaking
partial face
reeking of smoke

teeth and bone
lead-shattered
arms uncomfortably wrapped
around the carved
stock of the rifle

he was sick
from stink and sadness
touched nothing
called the police

***

the paramedics worked
slowly
unhurried
placing the old man
on a gurney
in a black bag
he told the police
the little he knew
as the ambulance
pulled away
without lights or sirens
gravel pinging the wheelwells

***

he found her name on
a letter marked
return to sender in a drawer

in the old man's room
just a daughter long gone
who called him a bastard
who wondered how he'd
gotten her number
who told a story about the
old man breaking a bag of
marbles in a rage when she
was just six turning her
favourite one to dust when
mom had finally had it and
left and took her away
for good
who called him a bastard
again not as loudly
asking him if a bastard
like that deserved any
better than dying alone
and again in a whisper
hanging up the phone
bastard…

***

he sat in his truck
waiting for the oppressive
heat to set
with the sun
behind the cedars

night came
before he worked up
the courage to get his shovel
and drag the dog
behind the house
where
he found
a fitting plot

he dug
with ease
a breeze starting to stir
gently whispering through
the trees
drying his brow
pushing a line of clouds
across orion's
belt

he dug
through topsoil
and soft earth
a shallow grave
for a stranger's
dog he never knew
gently rolling the body down
into the pit
where it lay
peaceful
in its decay
the moon catching its eyes and teeth

turning them white
for just an instant
before the first
shovel load

***

tomorrow he would
mend his fence

tomorrow he would come back
with a proper marker
made of one inch
pine
wondering what he should inscribe
on the crossbeam
for the stranger

wondering what a daughter would inscribe
on a headstone
for the bastard

R L R

About the Author

R L Raymond is simply a storyteller.

His work appears here, there and everywhere
in print and online journals.

He lives in Canada.

This is his first collection.

PigeonBike Press
www.PigeonBike.com
Canada 2011